Frankly Speaking

Inspiration for the Emerging Writer & Others

Written by Winona Rasheed

FRANKLY SPEAKING

(Inspiration for the Emerging Writer)

ISBN-13: 9781508969525

Published by Sugarberry Press

Acknowledgement: Cover Image Attributed to Freedigitalphotos.net and Aleksa D.

"The Journey of a passionate writer begins with big dreams, determination and small steps until you kick the door open."

Winona Rasheed

Introduction

Warrior of the Mighty Pen!

I am, I am!

Well, I did it again, thoughts running around in my head, keeping me awake and restless as a new project emerged in my head at 2 a.m. Yes, when inspiration hits, it doesn't care what time it is. All you know is that you just have to go with it. Let your thoughts flow!

So, this morning, here I sit trying to put it all together on paper-the vision which caused me to lose sleep. Only this time, the vision did not include characters, dialogue, plot or an engaging story line that develops from scratch. It seems my writing spirit is pulling me into another realm, that of nonfiction. My guardian angel, my inner spirit telling me to use my experience as a writer in a way to create a writing resource book for others that gives encouragement, self confidence and inspiration; an inspirational book that shows my determination, dedication and risk taking as I embarked on this journey. Stepping out there and getting my feet wet in the literary world and beyond, because this is what I do. This is me! I write and I create. I learn- experience and then I pass it on, because I just can't keep it to myself.

What I really want you to know is that this book isn't just for new and emerging writers; it's for anyone who needs a little uplifting, inspiration and encouragement; just because I enjoy helping others and because I think this book is a good thing.

So, here's my story.

My passion for writing began a long

time ago as a teenager. I wrote short stories in

certain classes for extra credit to boost my

grade and my self confidence. But the main

thing is I just enjoyed being creative. Too bad

my creativity did not help me when it came to

math, which was my least liked subject. For some reason, numbers were mind boggling.

But, I felt good when I was writing. So that must have been my calling, because I never let go of it. However, I did put it on the back burner for awhile as I pursued other things that were of interest to me as I became older and more independent; doing such things as holding down real paying jobs to support myself after my high school days; taking on the responsibilities of becoming an adult. In those early years, my mind was on making money, finding out what I wanted to do with my life, which included getting married and raising a family. I accomplished those things.

While accomplishing my goals and trying to figure out what to do with myself, I still managed to write here and there. It was hard staying focused with little ones running around. I suppose that back then, I wrote for therapeutic reasons. Writing was stuck in my head even though I didn't know how to go about having anything published. I had a strong desire to become published because I

thought my works were good enough and

because neighborhood people who were older

than myself would always say, "You should

have this published" after they read

something that I wrote. That was

encouragement to me.

You see, even though I wrote all those

stories in class for extra credit; not one

teacher showed me how, or instructed me in

the right direction to hone my craft. They

didn't even mention becoming a published

author. All I can say to that is- maybe they didn't know themselves. Maybe they didn't know just how serious and dedicated I was to my dream. Maybe, they didn't know I even had that dream. Maybe, they just didn't know my passion because I didn't speak up or ask questions. All I know was the fact that no one volunteered any input, suggestions or encouragement for me to pursue writing, except for the folks in the neighborhood. Maybe the educators thought the higher grade was good enough. Maybe they thought I would never do anything with the talent and didn't want to waste their time. Perhaps, they even figured that if I was serious enough, I'd seek my answers on my own; finding my little nook and move forward with it, seeking what I wanted to know if I was…..serious enough. Well guess what, I was serious enough! That's why I am eager to pass it on. Pass the inspiration on to others who might have the same passion either in writing and becoming an author with published books, or anyone who is struggling and chasing after their dreams. Trust me, the doors will open if you are patient enough, serious enough and when you start to believe in yourself....strive, strive, strive! It is important; no, it is vital that you do not give up. You can't and won't succeed if you do not push forward and stay focused, keeping your eye on the prize. It doesn't matter how long it may take to get there, the main thing is finally being able to say that you have arrived. That's a good feeling of accomplishment. I know this to be true because I've been there. That's why I am passing my experience on to you in this little book; showing what it means to be diligent in finding and working with your passion.

Some goals and dreams are not accomplished over night, and yes, sometimes the ideas that we have planted in our minds are not even meant to surface and come alive for some reason or another. For instance, at one time in my life I thought I wanted to be become a singer; all because I sounded good in the church choir. That was not my calling. Thank goodness because the thought of performing on stage to a crowd of people makes my knees wobble; even though being young, me and some female friends of mine had a girl's group going on. Yep, I was the

[15]

lead. All I can say to that, 'Sasha Fierce' I am not! After all, I am too laid back and I don't like being in the spotlight. I cringe at the thought.

While finding my nook, there was a time where I was thinking and believing that what I wanted to do was to become a nurse; after starting out as a nurse's aide. After all, I do enjoy helping others. However, that four year experience showed me that I was not cut out for that because I also had to deal with death when it occurred. That part of being in the medical field took the sparkle right out of nursing for me. I couldn't handle it.

Finding myself and my little nook in life also led me down another path, which I thought would be a lifelong career in the educational system, working with children. After all, children are uplifting and inspirational. Kids put that 'umph' in your life. That five year experience inspired me to do for self, inspiring me to want to own and operate my own in-home day care center, becoming an entrepreneur with my own little business. I wanted to be in charge of everything because I had the know-how, the experience and the education for working with young folk. I was ready, willing and able to do my own thing. But, God had other plans for me and in a subtle way; he told me that this fly by night dream would not manifest itself as I kept trying to open the door. There were obstacles that would not move or budge. Yes, I was very disappointed. However, over time, my guardian angel showed me the reasons why and today I thank God that that dream was just a passing fancy, because it allowed me to do what I am meant to do…..become a writer, creating books for young children, teens and those in between.

The lessons in life have bought me full circle and over stumbling blocks; leading me back home to my heart's desire, causing me to pick up my pen and write……my destiny, my purpose. Back to my roots because this obsession never left me even though I ventured off in other directions that were not meant to be. I am glad that I am back and doing me; after all these years, it is a glorious experience because I came back to my heart's desire. For what I do today, I am at peace with myself. As I believe, it's better late than never to claim your purpose and when you do, run with it! Engulf your whole being into it! Then sit back and enjoy the ride.

From the days of writing short stories for extra grading points, to the very first time that my mother and I tried to have a story published, which turned out to be a disaster because the publisher wanted hundreds of dollars up front to publish the book. Was this what it would be like to become an author?

SEEK AND YE SHALL FIND:

Eventually, I ended up going to school, learning the ropes and getting all the tools that I didn't have before when it came to writing, editing and publishing. I also learned the difference between vanity presses, which charge an arm and leg and the real deal publishers who chose to publish your works free of charge because of the worthiness and potential of your manuscript. Your written story, what a feeling you get when you receive an acceptance letter and legitimate documents that require your signature as you sign your name on a publishing contract. It is even far more wonderful when you go from a manuscript to seeing a sample book cover from the publisher showing the possibilities of your hard work and dedication. You get an exuberant feeling that you have finally arrived. That is hard to top! This event keeps you pressing forward for more. At least that is how it affects me, so I am testifying! I am doing a spiritual dance up in here!

Pursuing my purpose and holding on to my dreams have taken me down many roads leading to other adventures of the literary world; but not before I had a little education and experience in my background. There was a backup system put into place. I am so glad to have had it because it helped me to excel. It helped me to weed out the dumb stuff, the unnecessary things as took off on my journey.

Don't get me wrong, this journey is not an easy road to travel, but if you want it, you have to stay on the path regardless.

I first started out submitting my works or manuscripts to traditional publishing houses, the high ranking ones, the big name ones by way of postal mail.

I researched publishers by using an annual book catalog of publishing houses, making a list of publishers accepting material for children and teen story ideas; following their guidelines for submission. To that, all I can say is that just because you submit and you wait weeks or months on end does not mean just because you write well you are going to be accepted. When that happens, you don't give up hope....you press on. Thank goodness there are other avenues today for publishing your gems; like submitting through email, which seems to be a tad bit quicker when it comes to waiting on a response or simply… doing it yourself.

Perhaps, instead of trying to get that connection, or that 'foot in the door' with a big name publisher, take another route, such as using a small publishing house. This is where my break began. Like I said before, it has always been my dream to have what I have written published. I wanted a publisher to want and accept my work. I wanted to receive an acceptance letter, because to me it showed my worth as a writer. It gave me confidence and validation in what I was doing; showing that what I was doing was real and legit. I believed that this was the only way to go when it came to holding the title of author. But I was wrong! Out of 19 published books, 5 of them have been published by small publishing houses, publishers accepting work from writers who write for children and teens. My first contract, I was on cloud 9!

One publisher in particular really went over and beyond when they worked with me and my material and getting it in book form. They are my mentors in writing, editing and publishing to this very day. They took little ole me under their wings and showed me the ropes of publishing; passing on to me, their experience and know-how. They have left a big impression on me and my writing spirit. I was truly blessed to find a publisher who was not only encouraging, but one who believed in me and my potential. Three books published by them that became best sellers on Amazon.com. Even though I am no longer with this awesome, sweetheart of a publisher; to this very day, I can call upon them for advice, input, suggestions about writing and publishing. They are my backbone, a true friend. I don't think this type of relationship would have happened with a big name publisher. The three books that were published would probably still be in a queue somewhere as manuscripts waiting to be read, or worse yet….not accepted for publishing. I'd still be at the beginning line waiting for takeoff.

So, my hat goes off to New Line Press; an angel of a publisher because they also taught me that it is perfectly okay to self publish; be your own publisher. That's how Sugar Berry Book Press came about.

 **Sugarberry Books** That's all me!

Doing my thing and loving every minute of it.

Other things which I benefitted from when it comes to writing, editing and publishing are the opportunities and lessons that came about when I started following the desires of my heart, soul and spirit. Doors opened that I never even imagined, but guess what....I walked right on in, taking the risk. I absorbed everything that was put before me, because there was a lesson in it. It gave me hands on experience and I liked the idea of having a title before my name-**Managing Editor, Winona Rasheed.** That to me was pretty classy and my responsibilities gave me importance as I looked over, edited, managed and assigned incoming manuscripts with a website for writer/authors; handling writer's gems from all over the world. I got a taste of the publishing world and what it was like. I took part in helping others achieve their dreams of being published. I've read, edited and helped publish the works of online authors, giving them substance, meaning and importance as they seen their names and titles published on line. They got that little push that they needed.

This experience, opportunity and lessons helped me to develop and operate my own writing and editing business, **Dream Writers' Essentials**- helping writers prepare their manuscripts for submission. It gave me the experience to dabble in ghostwriting too. I was actually running a little business. It also set me on the path of becoming a freelance writer, writing articles for websites and individuals.

Yes, I am finally in my core, not only writing to benefit myself, but others too. An entrepreneur doing her own thing, having my own, a CEO you can say. I am pleased that I had this experience and the opportunities. I don't know what will come next in this literary world. Whatever it is and when it happens I will be ready for it. I will grab and fly with it because this is me. This is what I love. This is my calling and what I do best.

Speaking of what I do best, I will continue on my journey in self-publishing with Sugarberry Books. It is a fascinating world that I live in as writer/author. The opportunity is there for the taking, not just for me, but for those seeking to have their works published. You no longer need that affirmation of being accepted by a traditional publisher to have a published book. Accept yourself, validate yourself. Write it, edit it, and publish it! See it, claim it, accept your worth and then see it in print. Go forward and never ever believe that it can't or will not happen; grab all the opportunities and lessons that come your way, not only in publishing and writing, but with anything that you pursue with a passion. Hold on to the people that help you reach your dream and show you how to get there, especially the ones who take you under their wings and believe in you.

Hands on experience can go a long way and know that you do not always need a degree, (though it does look good and it makes you feel proud). Your guardian angel doesn't necessarily have to have a PHD or be a professor educating you in how to accomplish your goals and dreams. Pay attention to the ordinary person because they might be unique, special and very worthwhile in helping you to get to where you are going. They could be passing along encouragement…just like me.

Inspiration is Contagious, Pass it On!

Advice for the Writer in You

- Never underestimate yourself.

- Do not quit or give up.

- Edit, edit & edit your work before you submit, especially when you self-publish. Keep in mind that a self published author is not only a writer, but will have to become a developmental editor, substantive editor, copyeditor and a proofreader when they create a worthwhile book.

- Read all kinds of resources to help you master your craft. Information is at your finger tips.

- Drafts are your friends. Never think that just because you finished the story that it is done. You might have to go over it 100 times to make it perfect and right.

- There's nothing wrong with self-publishing. It has become quite popular in the 21st century, giving you all the tools you need to have a book.

- Be very leery of vanity presses- you should never have to pay a publisher to publish your work.

- Read, read, read. Write, write and write a little everyday!

- One important factor of writing is showing your story and not telling it. Chose the right words, for telling is not permitted.

- Welcome constructive criticism with an open mind.

- Stay away from those pesky little verbs because they are a nuisance in writing.

- Write/publish because it's a passion and not because you expect to get paid big bucks, though the royalty checks do put a smile on your face.

- There are plenty of resources on line pertaining to writing and editing and publishing, dive into researching all about it.

- Once you are published, keep in mind that your book needs to be promoted…that's your job! Don't slack in this area. Run with it and keep on running!

- Every writer/author needs a professional looking website for promoting your book and yourself.

- Did you know that social media sites such as Facebook, Twitter and Google+ are great places to promote your work and reach the masses of people? Sign up.

- Writing and blogging goes hand in hand. This too is another avenue for promoting.

- Receiving a rejection letter from a publisher does not mean that you are a terrible writer, or that you are not qualified to write and create. Get over it because some of the best well known writers have been rejected for some reason or another. Move on and be persistent. Don't give up!

- Do not bore your readers with lifeless characters, plots and dialogue, for the action of the book must stimulate the reader; make it lively, stimulating and unforgettable. Know your targeted audience.

- **It's never too late to begin your journey. Live, learn experience and wrap yourself in your desires if you are passionate enough to obtain them.**

Proof, I Have Arrived!

I did it! I accomplished it!

Along Came Jelly-Beanz
Winona Rasheed

The Race is On!

Winona Rasheed

[49]

Spring, Where Are You?
Winona Rasheed

Itchy

Scratchy Spots

written by Winona Rasheed

Illustrated by Penelope Dunn

I love Amazon because all of my 19 books are there!

Quotes to Live By

1) "First find out what your hero wants, then follow him!"   *Ray Bradbury*

2) "It is the writer who catches the imagination of young people, and plant a seed that will flower and come to fruition." *Issac Asimov*

3) "Writing is its own reward." *Henry Miller*

4) "I felt that I had to write. Even if I had never published, I knew that I would go on writing, enjoying it and **experiencing the challenge.**" Gwendolyn Brooks

5) "There is no greater agony than bearing an untold story inside you." *Maya Angelou*

6) "Putting words on paper regularly is part of the necessary discipline of writing." *Pearl Cleage*

Frankly Speaking, I hope you have been

inspired by this little book.

"I Love What I Do"